Fountain Shoppe™

fun ice cream recipes

by Robert Zollweg

Written and Designed by Robert Zollweg
Photography by Rick Luettke, www.luettkestudio.com
Graphics by Gary Raschke and Robert Zollweg
Art Direction Gary Raschke

Library of Congress Cataloging-in-Publication Data:

Fountain Shoppe
Fun Ice Cream Recipes / Robert Zollweg

ISBN 978-0-615-73302-9

Printed in the United States
R.R.Donnelley and Company

This book is dedicated to my two very special children,

Christopher and Rhonda

and their families, Doug, Sandy, Kaylie, Andrew, Bret, Morgan and Korrin.

To my mother, Virginia and to my wonderful and understanding family,
Richard & Sandy, Elaine & Tom, Judy & Carl
and all their children.

A special dedication to Steven and Annie

A very special thanks to Gary Raschke.
Without his help and guidance, his graphic knowledge, his art direction,
his patience, I'd still be working on this book.

To Rick Luettke, my photographer. He's the best in the business.

And to my loyal friend, Bill Muzzillo, for all his excellent editing skills.

To all my Libbey associates,
Karen Barentzen, Beth Baroncini, Cathie Logan, Kelly Kelley,
Denise Grigg, Gina Bacardi, Tom Fratantuono, Serena Williams,
Roger Williams, Jeff Joyce, Joe Mefferd, Greg Pax,
Fran Brietner, Vicki Richardson, Amy Lewarchik, Brooks Clayton,
Jennifer LaPlante, Sandy Shultz, Melissa Fleig and Emily West.

and to Libbey Glass, a great company.

Table of Contents

Introduction

What can you say about ice cream that hasn't been said a thousand times before? It's refreshing, delicious and not very healthy, but there are some things in life that are just too good to go without.

Ice cream has always been a family favorite. Kids love it and so do most adults. There are so many fun and different glass dishes that just make it all the more enjoyable. Your kids will love the fun party ideas, which are perfect for birthday parties as well as a special little treat when they finish their homework on time.

Ice cream makes a special little dessert when time is important. A small dish of ice cream or sorbet is perfect after a delicious dinner or when you want a little something sweet to finish off the evening.

Serving ice cream in special glass dishes just makes ice cream taste better.

Enjoy ! Robert Zollweg

History
and
Trivia

History of Ice Cream

The words ice cream are derived from earlier iced cream or cream ice which is a frozen dessert usually made from dairy products (milk and cream) and often combined with fruits and other ingredients or flavorings. Some countries call it frozen custard, sorbet or gelato.

In 400 BC, the Persians developed a dessert with snow and fruit juices; the Chinese around 200 BC had a frozen milk and rice dessert which was combined with fruit. So it can probably be said that ice cream dessert is the oldest known dessert in the world.

Ice cream as a dairy product was introduced in the 1600's in the United States by the Quaker colonists who brought their ice cream recipes from Europe.

The first ice cream parlor, or soda shop (as they were later known in America), opened in New York City in 1776. The colonists were the first to use the term ice cream from the original term iced cream.

In 1846, Nancy Johnson of Philadelphia was issued the first U.S. patent No. 3254 for a small scale hand-cranked ice cream freezer that is still in use today. In 1851, Jacob Fussell in Baltimore established the first large-scale commercial ice cream plant. Alfred Cralle patented the first ice cream scoop on February 2, 1897 and in 1926, Clarence Vogt invented the first commercially continuous process freezer for making ice cream for the masses.

Kelseigh, Saugatuck Drug (soda fountain est. 1913) in Saugatuck, Michigan

The ice cream sundae originated in the late 19th century. Legend has it that the ice cream soda was forbidden on Sunday because of the "Blue Laws," so the ice cream sundae was created to be able to serve ice cream on Sunday.

Several food vendors claimed to have invented the ice cream cone at the 1904 World's Fair in St. Louis, Missouri. Vendors ran out of cardboard dishes, so they used the Syrian waffles, rolled them into cones and a new product was born. But the Europeans were eating ice cream from a shell-like cone or pastry long before 1904.

Italo Marchiony sold his homemade ice cream from a push cart on Wall Street in New York City. To reduce his overhead caused by customers breaking or wandering off with his serving glasses, he developed the first edible waffle cups with sloping sides and a flat bottom and patented this idea on December 15, 1903 with the U.S. Patent No. 746971.

Modern day refrigeration greatly increased the popularity and reduced the cost of ice cream, making it readily available and affordable.

Soft serve ice cream was developed around the mid 1940's by a British chemical research team that included the young Margaret Thatcher. They figured out a way to double the amount of air in ice cream which allowed manufacturers to use less of the actual ingredients thus reducing costs. The soft serve ice cream machine, in which a cone is filled beneath a spigot, established or pioneered some major chain establishments today known as Dairy Queens, Carvel and Tastee Freez.

The 1980's saw a return of thicker or creamier premium ice creams like Ben and Jerry's and Haagen Dazs.

Ice Cream Facts and Trivia

Vanilla is the world's favorite flavor of ice cream, followed by Chocolate, then Butter Pecan, Strawberry, Neapolitan and Mint Chocolate Chip.

Ronald Reagan made July the official National Ice Cream month in 1984.

The first ice cream parlor opened in New York City in 1776 and the first ice cream ad appeared in print in 1777.

More ice cream is sold on Sunday than any other day of the week.

The most popular ice cream topping is chocolate, followed closely by whipped cream.

Kansas once had a ban on serving ice cream with cherry pie. Imagine that.

Margaret Thatcher was part of a team of chemists who invented soft serve ice cream before she became prime minister of England.

98% of all American households buy ice cream.

Children ages 2 to 12 and adults over 45 eat the most ice cream.

80% of all ice cream sales are sold in 1/2 gallons.

Ice cream is said to be the most popular dessert in the world.

Americans consume the most ice cream, followed by New Zealand, Denmark, Australia, Belgium, Sweden, Canada, Norway, Ireland and Switzerland.

The first ice cream parlor opened in New York City in 1776.

In 1983, Cookies 'N Cream ice cream became an instant hit and climbed to number five of the best selling ice creams.

In 1991, Chocolate Chip Cookie Dough was created.

Reuben Mattus invented Haagen Dazs in 1960. He choose the name because it sounded Danish.

In 1920, Harry Burt invented the Good Humor Ice Cream Bar and patented it in 1923. Burt sold his Good Humor bars from a fleet of white trucks with bells and uniformed drivers.

Chris Nelson invented the Eskimo Pie bar in the spring of 1920 and the first Eskimo Pie chocolate covered ice cream bar on a stick in 1934.

Americans eat more ice cream in the winter months than in the summer.

The traditional ice cream cone became popular during the St. Louis World's Fair in 1904.

Sherbet is made with 1-2% milk fat and is sweeter than ice cream.

Sorbet is made with fruit puree and has no dairy products in its ingredients.

Fun Glassware
and
Serving Suggestions

Fun Glassware for Serving

There are many wonderful glass dishes in the marketplace today that are perfect for serving all of your favorite ice cream and ice cream desserts. Let your imagination run wild. This book will show you all of my favorite ones and a few outside the box when it comes to serving suggestions.

I've used martini and margarita glasses, and even a red wine glass. Each makes a great sundae dish. Try a few scoops of sorbet in a champagne flute!

Be creative. There are many choices for serving ice cream. The containers seen in this volume can be purchased from various retailers.

Ice Cream Dishes

Sorbets and Ices

This glassware is perfect for small portions of sorbets, gelatos and flavored ices. Great for kids, too!

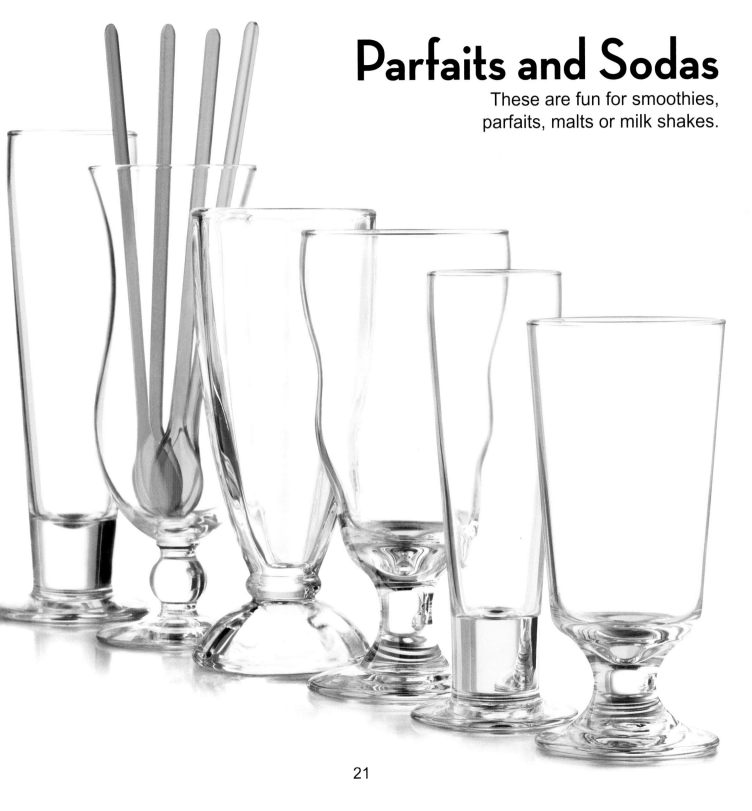

Parfaits and Sodas

These are fun for smoothies, parfaits, malts or milk shakes.

Serving Presentations - home party

A simple dessert buffet using a variety of different desserts makes the perfect ice cream party. Use flavored teas, dessert coffees and brandies to compliment your ice cream desserts. This will be a wonderful presentation when served a little later in the evening, after dinner or when you have finished playing cards or a favorite family game. Nothing beats ice cream desserts and a hot beverage.

birthday party

Here's another festive presentation for any birthday party or celebration. It can be adapted for kids by using goofier toppings and sprinkles. Adults may prefer the traditional toppings like chopped peanuts, hot fudge, etc. Use lots of different small bowls to hold all the different toppings as pictured above. Have several different sizes of dessert dishes for those who want just a little or a lot. Have a blender handy for malts or milk shakes. Let the kids or your guests just help themselves. It's easier for you and they will love it.

Simple Sundaes

Tin Roof circa 1940

My mother used to talk about tin roof sundaes when she was a kid. I guess it is nothing more than a dish of vanilla ice cream with chocolate syrup and peanuts. But the name sounds interesting, so here you have it: the Tin Roof !

This will make enough for several sundaes.

1 quart vanilla ice cream
one container of chocolate syrup or hot fudge topping
1 cup peanuts

In a simple 6 oz ice cream dish, add a generous scoop of vanilla ice cream, cover with chocolate sauce and a heaping spoonful of peanuts. It's just that simple and just that delicious. Serve and Enjoy !

For something different, try using caramel sauce instead of chocolate sauce or both.

Praline Passion

There is something about the word pralines that just screams southern decadence. This dessert is that and much more. I always use a good quality creamy vanilla ice cream.

This recipe will make 3-4 small desserts

1 quart vanilla ice cream
1 jar caramel sauce or topping
1 cup chopped pecans
1 jar chocolate sauce, about 4 ounces
4 oz whipped topping, optional

In a tall glass dessert dish, add a small scoop of vanilla ice cream and press to flatten. Add a tablespoon of caramel sauce, layer of pecans and then drizzle some chocolate sauce. Add another layer of vanilla ice cream, then the caramel sauce, pecans and chocolate sauce. Finish it off with a large dollop of whipped topping. Serve immediately. Enjoy !

Another one of my favorites is to add sliced bananas before covering with caramel sauce.

Hawaiian Paradise

This is a very tropical and rich dessert, especially delicious with a fresh ring of pineapple. Small glass bowls or dessert dishes make a very pleasing presentation. See photo at right.

This recipe will make one dessert.

2 rings of sliced pineapple
1/4 cup fresh mango, cubed
1 maraschino cherry
large scoop of vanilla ice cream, softened slightly
2 tbsp brown sugar
1 tsp butter or margarine, melted
small amount of water

Mix the brown sugar and melted butter with a little water to form a thick syrup. Dip the pineapple rings in the syrup until well coated.

Place one pineapple ring in the bottom of the dessert dish. Use half the mango cubes on top. Cover with softened vanilla ice cream and flatten a little. Add another pineapple ring, the rest of the mango and drizzle with a little brown sugar syrup. Garnish with a maraschino cherry in the center. That's it. Quick and simple and delicious. Serve immediately. Enjoy !

Famous Hot Fudge Sundae

There is nothing more delicious than a hot fudge sundae. Making it in a beautiful glass ice cream dish makes it all the more special. I use the tulip sundae dish, but any beautiful ice cream dish will work.

This recipe will make one sundae

2 scoops of vanilla ice cream
1/4 cup hot fudge
1 tbsp pecans, finely chopped, optional
whipped topping
maraschino cherry

In a glass dessert dish, place one scoop of vanilla ice cream. Add half the hot fudge topping. Then add another scoop of vanilla ice cream and finish it with the rest of the hot fudge. Add a large dollop of whipped topping and a maraschino cherry. Serve immediately. Enjoy !

Strawberry Festival

This one is quick and simple but very tasty. Fresh, ripe strawberries at the peak of the season just make this extra delicious. Try adding a slice of angel food cake before adding the ice cream and strawberries. You'll be surprised that it's so delicious.

Slightly softened ice cream is so much creamier. It really brings out the flavor of the fresh berries.

This will make two desserts in the large supreme sundae dishes. See photo at right.

1 cup fresh strawberries, sliced
1/2 cup fresh blueberries
one pint vanilla ice cream, softened
some whipped topping
two slices of angel food cake, optional

(You can also substitute some fresh sliced peaches, raspberries, pineapple, blueberries, mango, etc.)

In a glass dessert dish, start with a slice of angel food cake. Then add some strawberries and a few blueberries. Then a scoop of ice cream and then the sliced strawberries. Finish it off with a large dollop of whipped topping. Serve and Enjoy !

Traditional Ice Cream Sundae

Why even mention a simple everyday ice cream sundae? Every generation needs to know where it all started. It's pretty simple but still the most famous of all.

This will make several ice cream sundaes.

1/2 gallon of your favorite flavor of ice cream
some toppings: chocolate syrup, hot fudge, strawberry, caramel, etc.
some whipped topping
several maraschino cherries, optional
some sugar or vanilla wafers, optional

In an ice cream sundae dish, start with a small scoop of ice cream, then some of your favorite toppings. More than one is ok. Add another scoop of ice cream and more toppings. Complete it with a large dollop of whipped topping and a maraschino cherry. I like to serve it with sugar wafers. Serve and Enjoy !

Ice Cream Desserts

Ice Cream Cake

This is definitely one of our family favorites. I borrowed this recipe from Elaine Bender. She has been making this for years and it is very popular at all our family get togethers and birthday celebrations.

You can use any flavor of cake or ice cream. Try white cake with strawberry ice cream or chocolate cake with either chocolate chip, black cherry or chocolate mint ice cream. Each one makes a uniquely different ice cream dessert.

1 box cake mix (any flavor)
3/4 gallon ice cream, slightly softened
32 oz whipped topping (it comes in regular, chocolate and strawberry flavor)

Bake the cake mix in 2 round or square cake pans according to the package. Let cool.

Place the first layer of the cake on a footed serving platter. Evenly spread the ice cream to cover the layer of cake. Add the second layer of cake. Fluff the whipped topping with a spoon. Cover the entire 2 layer cake with whipped topping. Put in the freezer until set. Cover it with plastic wrap. You can make this a few days ahead if you are having a birthday party.

When ready to serve, remove from freezer about 30 minutes before serving. It will make cutting into slices a lot easier.

Pictured on the right is a chocolate cake with creamy strawberry ice cream in the center. Covered with whipped topping and garnished with fresh strawberries. Serve and Enjoy !

Mint Chocolate Chip Dessert

This is a delicious ice cream dessert I borrowed from my sister-in-law, Sandy, who has been making it for years. If you like mint and chocolate, you are going to love this dessert.

You can make it in a standard pie pan or individually in smaller ice cream dishes. Either way, it's delicious.

This recipe will make 6 individual desserts. See photo at right.

one package chocolate graham crackers, crushed
1/4 cup honey
1 quart mint chocolate chip ice cream, softened
1 cup chocolate mint cookies, crushed or broken into small pieces
1/2 cup chocolate fudge topping

In a mixing bowl, add the crushed chocolate graham crackers and the honey. Mix well. Sometimes I use a plastic sandwich bag to mix this up and it is easy for clean up.

In your dessert dishes, add about 2 tablespoons cracker crumbs. Now add a large scoop of ice cream, flatten down. Add layer of crushed chocolate mint cookies. Now another layer of ice cream. Add a tablespoon of chocolate fudge topping and sprinkle with a few pieces of the crushed chocolate mint cookies. These can be served immediately or covered with plastic wrap and put in the freezer until ready to use. Remove from freezer at least a half an hour before ready to serve. Enjoy !

Baked Alaska

The Chinese had the first idea for this dessert using pastry, but it was the French who added the meringue and made the actual first Baked Alaska, which they called omelette norvegienne or Norwegian Omelette. In the U.S., the name Baked Alaska was coined at Delmonico's Restaurant in 1876 to honor the acquisition of the Alaskian territory and February 1st is Baked Alaska Day in the United States. Variations of this dessert have been made over the years and here is another one that is quite simple and delicious.

This recipe will make 6 individual desserts, served in mini pie plates. See photo at right.

1 quart pistachio ice cream, softened
1 cup graham cracker crumbs
2 tbsp sugar
one 16 oz container of whipped topping

1 pound cake, sliced
2 tbsp butter or margarine
1/4 cup chopped pistachios

Mix the cracker crumbs, sugar and melted butter in a mixing bowl. Place about 2 tablespoons of cracker mixture in the bottom of the baking dish and press down. Baked these in an oven at 350 degrees for 10 minutes. Let cool. Place a slice of pound cake on top of the cracker crust. Cover with softened pistachio ice cream. Add a large dollop of whipped topping and sprinkle with chopped pistachios. Serve and Enjoy !

For a Neapolitan version of this recipe, replace the pistachio ice cream with strawberry, chocolate and vanilla ice creams. Follow the recipe from above. Serve and Enjoy !

Party Ring Surprise

This is such a festive way to serve an ice crean sundae for a larger group of people or is ideal for a birthday party. It makes a great presentation and tastes just wonderful. You can make it with any flavor of ice cream, although when using vanilla ice cream, you can see all the layering and center fillings.

You will need one glass or metal ring pan, some plastic wrap and all the ingredients listed below.

1 gallon ice cream (any flavor) softened
some ice cream toppings (chocolate syrup, hot fudge, caramel, strawberry, etc.)
4 oz toffee pieces, mini chocolate chips, chopped peanuts or pecans
some plastic wrap

Using a glass or metal ring pan, moisten with water. Line the ring pan with plastic wrap. Place in freezer for 10 minutes so the plastic wrap really clings to the pan. Fill the ring pan about half full with the softened ice cream, smooth down. Add any condiments you like. I like to add hot fudge, caramel and chopped pecans. Cover or fill the remaining ring pan with ice cream. You can even use two different kinds of ice cream, like chocolate on the bottom and vanilla on the top as pictured on the right.

Place ring pan in freezer for a few hours. When ready to serve, remove from freezer, let stand a few minutes and gently lift the ice cream dessert out of the pan using the plastic wrap. Place upside down on the flat surface of a cake plate or platter. Carefully remove the plastic wrap. Drizzle with a little topping and sprinkle with nuts or toffee pieces. Serve immediately. Store any leftovers in the freezer. Enjoy !

Ice Cream Parfait

This is a pretty simple ice cream dessert to make anytime. I love the chocolate version, but you can use different flavors of ice cream or fresh fruit.

This recipe will make two ice cream parfaits. See photo at right.

You will need:

four scoops of vanilla ice cream, softened
3 tbsp of chopped peanuts or pecans
3 tbsp of mini chocolate chips
1/4 cup of chocolate syrup
two dollops of whipped topping

OR

four scoops of vanilla ice cream, softened
1 cup of fresh sliced strawberries, blueberries and raspberries
two dollops of whipped topping

In a tall glass parfait glass, add a scoop of ice cream, then some peanuts, chocolate chips and some chocolate sauce. Add another scoop of ice cream and more peanuts, chocolate chips and chocolate syrup. Finish off with a large dollop of whipped topping. Serve immediately. Enjoy !

These are great made ahead of time, wrapped in plastic wrap and placed in the freezer until ready to use. Serve and Enjoy !

Apple Orchard A-la-mode

Here is an incredible version of the All American apple pie a la mode. Very simple and equally delicious. You can make the baked apples ahead of time, but the finished dessert should be served immediately.

This recipe will make 6 servings in a 7oz dessert dish. See photo at right.

5-6 fresh apples, peeled and sliced or chunked
1/2 cup brown sugar
1 tbsp butter or margarine
1/4 tsp cinnamon
dash of nutmeg
1 quart of vanilla ice cream
caramel sauce for topping
1/4 cup finely chopped pecans

In a microwaveable bowl, place the sliced or chunked apples. Add the brown sugar, butter and spices. Toss until well coated. Microwave for about 2 minutes until hot but crunchy.

Fill the bottom of each dessert dish with the baked apples. Add a scoop of vanilla ice cream on top and drizzle a little apple cinnamon sauce that is left over on top of the ice cream. Then drizzle with a little caramel sauce and sprinkle with pecan pieces. Serve immediately. Enjoy !

Chocolate Fantasy

Nothing is better than cake and ice cream. This magnificent dessert is rich and chocolatey. The recipe calls for using larger supreme sundae dishes, but you can make smaller mini-sundaes that are perfect for tasting parties.

The ingredients below will make enough for 6-8 desserts depending on what size pan of brownies you make or buy.

You will need several 4"-5" bowls. See photo at right.

several chocolate brownies
one quart chocolate or vanilla ice cream
chocolate sauce or chocolate fudge topping
6 oz whipped topping or whipping cream
1/2 cup chopped pecans or peanuts
several maraschino cherries

In a small round or square bowl, place a chocolate brownie. Now add a scoop of ice cream. Pour a heaping spoonful of chocolate syrup or fudge topping over the ice cream. Sprinkle with chopped nuts and a large dollop of whipped topping. Finish it off with a maraschino cherry. Serve and Enjoy !

Eleanor's Heavenly Delight

The Bender Family of Toledo, Ohio thought I should use this recipe in my next book because their mother made it for them for years and it is a family favorite. I hope you enjoy it as much as the Bender Family.

This recipe will make enough to fill 6 small dessert dishes. See photo at right.

1 small box of red gelatin
1 quart of vanilla ice cream, softened
2 cups water

(This dessert can be made with almost any flavor of gelatin.)

Boil 1 cup of water and mix with the red gelatin until completely dissolved. Add one cup cold water and mix thoroughly. Let set until thickened, but not set.

Add the softened vanilla ice cream to the gelatin and beat with an electric mixer until smooth. Divide equally into the small dessert dishes and refrigerate for an hour or so. Remove from refrigerator about 15 minutes before serving. Enjoy !

Snappy Fruit Cream Parfaits

This is another one of my healthy favorites. It's really delicious in the morning or for brunch and is very easy to prepare. This recipe is all about the glassware. Layered ice cream is normal, but layering it in a cool parfait glass really adds more pizzazz to the presentation, especially when you are entertaining.

You will need several parfait glasses, about 8-10 oz each. See photo at right.

16 oz vanilla yogurt or softened vanilla ice cream
8 oz granola
2 cups of mixed berries (blueberries, sliced strawberries and raspberries)

You can use almost any fresh fruit that can be cut into small pieces to fit into the parfait glass. Try pineapple, cantaloupe, raspberries, peaches, pears, raisins, etc.

Add a 1/2" layer of ice cream or yogurt to the bottom of the dessert dish. Now add fresh berries, some more yogurt or ice cream, more berries, a little more yogurt. Finish it off with a tablespoon of granola.

You can add the granola in layers but it tends to get soft and less crunchy. I usually put it on top to keep it crunchy.

Keep refrigerated. Serve and Enjoy !

Bananas Foster

This is one of my favorites and will definitely be a hit with all your dinner guests. Serve it with a nice glass of Pinot Grigio or a Riesling.

This recipe will make 4 servings. See photo at right.

1/3 cup butter or margarine	1/3 cup dark brown sugar
3 ripe bananas, sliced	1/4 tsp cinnamon
2 tbsp creme de cacao	1/2 cup dark rum
2 cups ice cream, softened	1/4 cup finely chopped pecans

In a large skillet, melt the butter, stir in the brown sugar until melted. Add the sliced bananas and gently stir on medium heat until well coated and heated through. Sprinkle with cinnamon. Stir in the creme de cacao. Set aside.

In a small saucepan, heat the rum over medium heat for about 10 minutes or until it simmers. Ignite the rum with a long fireplace match. Pour the rum into the bananas, mix well, until coated evenly.

Fill each of the 4 ice cream dishes with about a 1/2 cup of ice cream.

Spoon the warm banana and rum mixture over the ice cream and sprinkle with chopped pecans. Serve immediately. Enjoy !

Tiramisu

This may not be the real Italian dessert, but it is an ice cream version that will surely be as delicious as its counterpart. There are two different versions you can make from this one recipe. I usually make it in a 9x13 pan, but making it in individual dishes is wonderful and adds a lot more pizzazz when entertaining, especially for a tasting party.

This recipe will either make one 9x13 pan or 12 small ice cream dishes for individual servings. See photo at right.

4 cups of crumbled vanilla wafers
1/2 gallon of vanilla ice cream, softened
8 oz chocolate syrup
1/2 cup espresso or 2 tbsp instant coffee
1 bag (8oz) toffee pieces
1 bag (8oz) mini chocolate chips
8 oz whipped topping

This is a layered dessert, so whether it is in a 9x13 pan or in individual ice cream dishes, you will be layering the different ingredients.

In a 9x13 pan (or individual ice cream dishes), add a layer of crumbled vanilla wafers, and a layer of softened ice cream. Then mix the chocolate syrup and coffee together. Pour over ice cream. Sprinkle with toffee pieces and mini chocolate chips. Add another layer of ice cream. Finish off with a mixture of vanilla wafer crumbs, toffee pieces and mini chocolate chips. Cover the whole dessert with whipped cream or add a large dollop on each individual ice cream dish. This can be served immediately or put in the freezer for an hour or so until firm. When ready to serve, remove from freezer about 30 minutes before serving. Cut into squares and serve. Enjoy !

Homemade Chocolate Ice Cream

This is quick, easy, and you will be surprised how silky smooth this homemade ice cream can be. Even better, you will not need an ice cream freezer to make this.

This recipe will make about 2 quarts and can be served in any unusual ice cream dish. See photo at right.

4 cups whipping cream
14 oz can of sweetened condensed milk
16 oz chocolate syrup
1 cup chopped pecans or walnuts or peanuts, optional

For something different, try mini chocolate chips or crushed peppermint candy.

In a medium glass mixing bowl, combine the whipping cream, sweetened condensed milk, and chocolate syrup. Beat with an electric mixer until soft peaks form. Add any extra ingredients you want now. Fold in until well blended. Pour the mixture into a glass 8x8 pan and freeze about 8 hours or so until firm.

When ready to serve, remove from freezer for a few minutes, scoop out what you need and return to freezer, covered.

Serve in any special ice cream dish and Enjoy !

Eggnog Ice Cream Dessert

This particular dessert is creamy with vanilla ice cream, nutmeg and a pinch of rum. Adding pecans just makes it all the more delicious. Small serving containers is the ideal way to serve it to make it all the more special.

You will need 6 special ice cream dishes suitable for baking. See photo at right.

24 ginger snap cookies
1 cup chopped pecans, divided
1/4 cup butter or margarine, melted
1 quart French vanilla ice cream, softened
2 tsp nutmeg
2 tsp rum extract

In a blender, add the ginger snap cookies and half the pecans and process until finely ground. Add butter and process until mixed well and crumbly. Fill each glass ramekin with about a 1/4 inch of cookie mixture. Flatten and bake in oven at 350 degrees for 8-10 minutes. Remove from oven and let cool.

In a large mixing bowl, combine the softened vanilla ice cream, nutmeg and rum extract. Stir until well blended. Fill each of the dishes almost full with ice cream mixture. Cover each dish with chopped pecans.

Cover each dessert dish with a plastic lid or plastic wrap and place in freezer for 3-4 hours. Remove from freezer about 5-10 minutes before serving. Serve and enjoy !

Strawberry Pistachio Dessert

The creamy taste of strawberries and pistachio is just unbelievable. Serving this delicious ice cream dessert in special ice cream dishes just adds to the unique presentation. Sometimes I substitute Black Cherry ice cream instead of strawberry. Either one will really excite your taste buds.

You will need 6 ice cream dishes. See photo at right.

1 cup chocolate graham cracker crumbs
1/4 cup chopped pistachios or pecans or peanuts

1/4 cup powdered sugar
3 tbsp butter or margarine, melted

1 quart strawberry ice cream, softened
1 pkg (3.4 oz) instant pistachio pudding
1 jar of hot fudge topping, optional

1 quart vanilla ice cream, softened
3/4 cup half and half
3-4 strawberries for garnish, optional

In a mixing bowl, combine cracker crumbs, powdered sugar and chopped nuts. Add the melted butter and mix well. Place about 2 tablespoons of crumb mixture in the bottom of each dessert dish. Press down. Set aside.

Spoon softened strawberry ice cream over the crumb mixture. Smooth with the back of a large spoon. Put in freezer for 10 minutes or so.

In another large mixing bowl, add the softened vanilla ice cream, stir with spoon until creamy. In another small bowl, combine the pudding mix and half and half, stir until blended. Add to ice cream. Mix with an electric mixer on low speed until well blended. Spoon over strawberry ice cream. Return to freezer for 2-3 hours or until firm. When ready to serve, remove from freezer a few minutes ahead of time. Add a large dollop of hot fudge topping and a strawberry slice for garnish. Serve and enjoy !

Peanut Cream Surprise

This delicious chocolate and peanut fudgy dessert is bound to be a real hit with your family and friends at your next dinner party. These can be made ahead of time and put in the freezer. When ready to serve, remove from freezer about 10-15 minutes ahead of time. Place on a small plate and you are ready to go.

You will need 6 small square or straight sided dessert dishes. See photo at right.

1 cup chocolate graham cracker crumbs
1 cup mini chocolate chips, divided
1 quart vanilla ice cream, softened
1/2 cup chocolate fudge topping

2 tbsp butter or margarine, melted
1 cup peanuts, divided
1 jar caramel topping

You can also use chocolate ice cream if you really love chocolate.

In a mixing bowl, combine the cracker crumbs and melted butter. Mix until crumbly. Stir in half the mini chocolate chips and half of the peanuts, finely chopped. If you use the large chocolate chips, chop them up a little into smaller pieces. Fill the bottom of each dessert dish with about a 1/2" of this mixture. Set aside.

Then fill the dessert dish with vanilla ice cream and smooth with back of a large spoon. Spoon a large dollop of the chocolate fudge topping on top and spread around. Drizzle caramel sauce on top and cover with a layer of peanuts. You can use whole peanuts or chopped. Place in the freezer for an hour or so until ready to serve. They should be removed from freezer at least 5-10 minutes before serving. They are a little easier to eat when they are a little softer. Serve and enjoy !

Frozen Strawberry Lime Delight

The combination of strawberries and limes mixed with the smooth texture of yogurt is just about as good as it gets for a frozen dessert. The best part of all is that it's somewhat healthy. So enjoy it !

You will need 6 tall glass dessert dishes, see photo at right.

14 oz sweetened condensed milk (not evaporated)
3 containers (6 oz each) key lime yogurt
3 containers (6 oz each) strawberry yogurt
1 cup fresh strawberries, chopped
1 tbsp fresh lime zest, about 1 lime

In two mixing bowls, divide the sweetened condensed milk equally. Stir in the strawberry yogurt in one bowl and the key lime yogurt into the other. Mix each well. Fill each of the dessert dishes half full with the lime yogurt mixture. Add some strawberries and lime zest to each. Fill each dessert dish with the strawberry yogurt mixture until full. Place in the freezer for at least 6-8 hours until solid. Remove from freezer about 15 minutes before serving. Enjoy !

Chocolate Lovers Dream

Pecans, chocolate and bananas are a perfect combination when you want to over indulge in something really over the top. Don't worry about the calories or whether or not it is good for you. The Chocolate Dream is just that, something to dream about.

You will need several banana split dishes. This recipe will make about 4-5 desserts. See photo at right.

1 half gallon chocolate ice cream
4-5 bananas, sliced the long way
1/2 cup chocolate syrup
1/2 cup caramel syrup
1/2 cup finely chopped pecans
some whipped topping

If you want it a little less chocolatey, use vanilla ice cream.

Place 2-3 small scoops of ice cream in each dish. Place a sliced banana along each side. Drizzle chocolate syrup then caramel syrup over the ice cream. Sprinkle with chopped pecans. Finish off with a dollop of whipped topping. Serve and Enjoy !

Mocha Cream Dessert

What could be more delicious after a wonderful dinner than a heavenly dessert made with coffee and cream? It's a coffee lover's dream.

You will need 6 special dessert dishes. See photo at right.

10 whole graham crackers, broken up
1/2 cup dark brown sugar

1/2 cup butter or margarine, melted
1/2 cup chopped pecans

1 quart vanilla ice cream, softened
1 jar hot fudge topping
1/3 cup coffee flavored liqueur

1 quart coffee ice cream, softened
1 cup whipped topping

In a mixing bowl, combine cracker crumbs, melted butter, brown sugar and chopped pecans. Mix until well blended. Add a large spoonful to each dessert dish. Use about half of this mixture.

Fill each dessert dish about half full with vanilla ice cream. Drizzle a little hot fudge topping and add a layer of cracker mixture topped with another drizzle of hot fudge topping.

Fill each dessert dish with the coffee ice cream, leaving a little room for final layer. In another mixing bowl, combine the whipped topping and coffee liqueur. Mix well. Add a large dollop of this topping to each dessert dish. Place in freezer for about an hour or so, or serve immediately. Enjoy !

Italian Spumoni

Spumoni ice cream is always associated with Italian food. Traditionally, this dessert is made in a long loaf pan and sliced. I like making it in individual dishes because I can make it ahead of time and freeze it until ready to serve. I also like to sit on my porch on a warm summer evening with a bowl of this wonderful dessert. Delicious!

You will need 6 dessert dishes, something kind of tall to show off the layers of different flavors. See photo at right.

1 quart black cherry ice cream, softened
1 quart milk chocolate ice cream, softened
1 quart vanilla ice cream, softened
1 box (3 oz) pistachio instant pudding
1/4 cup chopped hazelnuts or pecans
1/4 cup chopped pistachios
1/4 cup mini chocolate chips or shaved chocolate
some whipped topping
several maraschino cherries

Fill each dessert dish about 1/3 full of chocolate ice cream. Sprinkle with chocolate chips and chopped hazelnuts. Place in freezer.

In a mixing bowl, add the softened vanilla ice cream and stir until creamy. Add the pistachio pudding powder and blend well. Spoon the pistachio ice cream on top of the chocolate ice cream to about 2/3 full. Sprinkle with chopped pistachios. Return to freezer.

Fill each dish with a scoop of black cherry ice cream. Finish off with a large dollop of whipped topping and a maraschino cherry. Serve immediately and Enjoy !

Banana Split Delight

Back when I was a kid, if you ordered a banana split at a soda fountain shop, this is what you got - a wonderful combination of chocolate, strawberry and vanilla ice cream with 3 different toppings and lots of whipped cream and a maraschino cherry of top. Back then it was the most over the top ice cream dessert on the menu. Probably still is, but worth every penny !

You will need 6 banana split dishes See photo at right.

1 quart chocolate ice cream
1 quart strawberry ice cream
1 quart vanilla ice cream
6 bananas, sliced the long way
1/2 cup chocolate syrup
1/2 cup strawberry topping
1/2 cup pineapple topping
some whipping cream or whipped topping
small jar of maraschino cherries

You can use almost any flavor of ice cream, but tradition has it with chocolate, vanilla and strawberry.

Start with a scoop of chocolate ice cream, then a scoop of vanilla and then a scoop of strawberry. Place a banana slice on each side of the dish. Put a spoonful of chocolate syrup over the chocolate ice cream, a spoonful of pineapple topping over the vanilla ice cream and finally, a spoonful of strawberry topping over the strawberry ice cream. Put a dollop of whipped topping on each scoop of ice cream and a maraschino cherry. Don't wait too long before you enjoy this delicious dessert. Serve and Enjoy !

Ice Cream S'mores

If, when you were a kid and you never experienced the wonderful taste of homemade S'mores while camping or sitting by the campfire, you missed out on something very special. Hopefully, you've tasted one. The combination of marshmallows and chocolate is really delicious.

You will need 6 banana split dishes for a dramatic presentation. See photo at right.

12 whole graham crackers
1 cup marshmallow creme
1/2 gallon chocolate ice cream, slightly softened
1 jar of hot fudge topping
1/2 cup mini chocolate chips
whipped topping for garnish, optional

Place several pieces of graham crackers in each dessert dish. Add a spoonful or two of hot fudge on top of the crackers. Add two scoops of chocolate ice cream. Flatten down. Add a spoonful of marshmallow creme on top of the ice cream. Another cracker or two. Press down slightly. Add another spoonful of hot fudge and a dollop of marshmallow creme on top. Sprinkle with mini chocolate chips. It will look rather gooey, but don't worry about how it looks. It will taste fabulous. Serve immediately. Enjoy !

Smoothies, Malts & Milk Shakes

Orange Delight Smoothie

An Orange Delight is just that, a deliciously smooth and subtle combination of orange and cream. Very refreshing and perfect when you are sitting on the patio in the middle of the afternoon, soaking up some sun.

This will make 2-3 smoothies in a 14-16 oz smoothie glass

1 quart vanilla ice cream
2 cups orange juice
2 cups crushed ice

In a blender, add the orange juice and crushed ice. Blend until frothy. Add the ice cream and blend until smooth. Serve in a tall smoothie or cooler glass. Enjoy !

Berry Cream Smoothie

Follow the recipe from above but add 1 cup of fresh berries (strawberries, raspberries or blueberries) before adding the ice cream. Serve and Enjoy !

Frozen Yogurt & Fruit Smoothie

Frozen smoothies are delicious and basically good and healthy. It all comes down to the ingredients. Both of these smoothie recipes contain healthy ingredients.

You will need 3-4 tall smoothie glasses for a fabulous presentation. See photo at right.

1 quart vanilla or plain yogurt
1 quart fresh strawberries
1 banana, sliced
2 cups crushed ice

In a blender, add the yogurt and crushed ice. Blend until chunky. Add the strawberries and banana slices. Blend until smooth. Pour into individual smoothie glasses, add a fat straw and you are ready to go. Enjoy !

Pineapple & Cream Smoothie

Follow the recipe from above but substitute the fresh strawberries with 2 cups fresh pineapple. Add the banana and process until smooth. Serve and Enjoy !

Pineapple & Coconut Smoothie

This is also known as a Pina Colada Smoothie, especially when you add a dash of rum. Either way, it is delicious and refreshing. The only thing you could add would be a trip to Aruba or Bermuda.

This will make 2-3 large smoothies in a tall glass. See photo at right.

1-1/2 cups pineapple juice
1/2 cup coconut milk
3/4 cup vanilla ice cream
1 cup frozen pineapple chunk, fresh or canned
1 cup crushed ice
2 tbsp fresh grated coconut for topping, optional

Pour the pineapple juice, crushed ice and coconut milk in a blender, blend a little. Add the ice cream and blend until smooth. Add the pineapple chunks and blend some more. Pour the mixture into tall skinny glasses and garnish with a pineapple wedge and shredded coconut on top. Serve and Enjoy !

Peach & Pineapple Smoothie

Follow the recipe from above but substitute 1 cup fresh or canned peaches (chopped) for the coconut milk. Serve and Enjoy !

Hawaiian Smoothie

This could be called a smoothie or a shake. Either way, you'll be on your way to Hawaii before you know it. Tropical flavored smoothies are refreshing and invigorating.

This recipe will make 3-4 servings in a tall smoothie glass. See photo at right.

1 cup fresh milk
3 tbsp coconut milk
1 cup ice cream
2 bananas, sliced and frozen
1 cup pineapple chunks, fresh or canned
1 papaya, seeded and diced
1 ripe mango, pitted, peeled and diced
1 cup crushed ice

Pour the milk, crushed ice and coconut milk into a blender and process gently until combined. Add half the ice cream and blend. Add the remaining ice cream and blend. Add the frozen banana slices, pineapple, mango and papaya and blend until smooth. Pour the mixture into the smoothie glasses. Serve and Enjoy !

Peppermint Smoothie

This one is very refreshing and perfect for the holidays. During the holiday season, hang a candy cane over the side of the glass for a fun garnish.

This recipe will make 2-3 servings in a tall smoothie glass. See photo at right.

1 cup milk
2 tbsp peppermint syrup
2 cups peppermint ice cream
4-5 crushed peppermint candies
1 cup crushed ice
a couple of candy canes or peppermint sticks for garnish

In a blender, pour the milk, crushed ice, peppermint candy and peppermint syrup. Blend gently. Add the peppermint ice cream half at a time and blend until smoothly blended. Garnish with a candy cane or peppermint stick. Serve and Enjoy !

Chocolate Mint Smoothie

Follow the recipe from above but add 1/4 cup of chocolate syrup to the recipe when adding the milk, candy, etc. for the first blending.

Silk & Smoothie Delight

This is a very smooth and refreshing dessert that is great at breakfast or brunch. These also make great after school snacks for the kids and can be made with almost any fruit.

This recipe will make 2-3 smoothies in the hurricane glass. See photo at right.

2 cups vanilla ice cream or vanilla yogurt
1 cup of whipping cream
1/2 cup whole milk
12 oz bag frozen mixed berries, thawed
1 cup crushed ice

To make a specific fruit flavor, just use 12 ounces of your favorite fresh or frozen fruit.

Slightly chop or puree the mixed berries in the blender. Add the yogurt, milk and crushed ice. Blend well. Add the whipped topping, puree until smooth and creamy. Pour into tall smoothie glasses.

These are light and fluffy. Kids will love them, adults too. Serve and Enjoy !

Tropical Mango Smoothie

This tropical smoothie has a unique flavor of fresh mango. Orange and pineapple have been around for ages, but mango is relatively new in the kitchen and may be slightly ahead of its time when it comes to fresh fruit. Try it and you'll be pleasantly surprised at the unique flavor it delivers. Be sure the mangos are ripe (they will feel kind of soft).

This recipe will make 2-3 smoothies in a tall glass. See photo at right.

2 cups orange mango juice
2 ripe mangos, peeled, pitted and diced
1 cup crushed ice
2 cups vanilla ice cream

In a blender, add the orange mango juice, crushed ice and the fresh mango pieces. Blend well. Add the vanilla ice cream half at a time and blend until smooth. Serve in very tall and skinny glasses. Enjoy !

Chocolate Milk Shakes

Nothing brings back those pleasant childhood memories like sitting on a swivel stool in a local ice cream shop and ordering a chocolate milk shake. It was so large that you could share it with a friend, but you usually drank the whole thing yourself.

For a different flavor, substitute the chocolate syrup for fresh strawberries or caramel.

This recipe will make one very large milk shake in a tall soda glass. See photo at right.

1 cup fresh milk
1 cup chocolate or vanilla ice cream
1/4 cup chocolate syrup
some whipped topping for garnish

In a blender, add all the ingredients and blend until rich and smooth. Serve in a tall, sleek soda glass. Finish off with a dollop of whipped topping. Enjoy !

Chocolate Malts

This delicious ice cream dessert is very similar to the shake and the only real difference is that you add a large scoup of malted milk powder.

Follow the recipe from above and add a large scoup of malted milk powder. Blend until smooth, Serve and Enjoy !

Sorbets & Ices

Italian Lemon Ice (Gelato di Limone)

Italian Ice is basically a flavored carnival snow cone. It sounds pretty simple and ordinary, but with the right ingredients, it is quite delicious and makes a wonderful palet cleanser between dinner courses or a light, healthy dessert.

You will need 6 small, glass dessert dishes that are perfect for serving flavored ices. See photo at right.

2 cups cold water
1-1/2 cups white sugar
grated lemon peel from one lemon
2/3 cup fresh lemon juice

In a saucepan, combine water, lemon peel and sugar and bring to a boil. Simmer for 10 minutes on a lower heat. Remove from heat and let mixture cool.

Add lemon juice to cooled syrup. It should taste like a very strong lemonade. Place in a air tight container suitable for freezing. Freeze until slushy. Beat with an electric mixer and refreeze for another few hours. This can be done once or twice. Serve in mini ice cream dishes. Enjoy !

Fresh Fruit Ice

This is ideal for a refreshing summer dessert or snack when you really want something a little sweet but very healthy. It's an ideal little dessert after a heavy dinner or to cleanse your palet during dinner courses.

This will make enough to fill 6 mini sorbet dishes. See photo at right.

You will need lots of crushed ice, about 4-6 cups
Any kind of fresh fruit (strawberries, raspberries, blueberries, pineapple, mango, peaches, etc,)
1/4 cup sugar or sugar substitute equivalent

Place the fresh fruit and sugar in a blender or food processor. Blend until pureed. Add the crushed ice and blend until crunchy.

Scoop into wonderful little sorbet type dishes and serve immediately. Enjoy !

Flavored Fruit Ice

This recipe is similar to the one above but you use flavored cocktail syrup instead of fresh fruit purees. Use any flavor of cocktail syrup. There are some wonderful flavors available today. You can make your own flavorings with a fresh fruit puree or concentrate fruit juices.

In a blender, add the crushed or chopped ice and blend until slushy. Add about 2 ounces of your favorite flavoring and blend until smooth. Scoop into small dessert dishes and serve immediately. Enjoy !

Homemade Tropical Sorbet

Sorbet is a lot like Italian Ice but uses a lot less water. It is pretty much pure frozen fruit juices. Very flavorful and delicious with a sugar wafer cookie on the side.

You will need about 6 small dessert or sorbet dishes. See photo at right.

1 cup fresh pineapple chunks
1 cup fresh mango, chunked
1 kiwi, peeled and sliced
1/4 cup orange juice
2 tbsp lemon juice
1 cup white granulated sugar

Place all the ingredients in a blender or food processor and blend until smooth. Make sure sugar is dissolved.

Place the pureed mixture in a metal pan or bowl with a lid. Place in freezer for about 3 hours until the edges are hard and the center is slushy. Remove from freezer and whisk until smooth. Return to freezer covered and freeze until firm, about 4 hours.

When ready to serve, spoon into small dessert dishes and serve immediately. Return any unused sorbet to freezer for another time. Enjoy !

Homemade Peach Sorbet

Peach and raspberry sorbets are my favorites. They are crisp and sweet and perfect when you need a little something sweet. In Michigan, August is the month for delicious and juicy ripe peaches and blueberries. Perfect for fresh homemade sorbet. Serve it in mini dessert dishes for a real flare in entertaining at a tasting party.

You will need several of these mini dessert dishes. See photo at right.

6-8 large ripe peaches, peeled and sliced
3 tbsp lemon juice
1/2 cup sugar or honey
2 tbsp corn syrup
1 cup water

In a saucepan, combine sugar, water and lemon juice. Cook over medium heat until sugar is completely dissolved. Remove from heat and let cool. Transfer to a blender and add the sliced peaches and corn syrup. Process until smooth. Pour into a metal pan and cover. Freeze for about 3 hours. Remove from freezer and whisk until smooth. Return to freezer for another 3-4 hours. When ready to serve, remove from freezer. Scoop into each of the mini sorbet dishes and serve immediately. Enjoy !

Homemade Blueberry Sorbet

Use the basic recipe from above but substitute the peaches with 5 cups fresh or frozen blueberries. Mash the blueberries and strain in a sieve to remove all skins. Process blueberries and syrup mixture until smooth. Freeze as directed. Garnish with some fresh blueberries. Serve and Enjoy !

Just for Kids !

Blue Lagoon

This is a real kid pleaser. It's shockingly blue and surprisingly delicious. Today's kids like things different and more out there. Blue Lagoon will definitely accomplish that.

This recipe will make one ice cream dessert in a long banana split dish. See photo at right.

2 scoops of vanilla ice cream
2 tbsp blue cocktail mix
1 banana, sliced
1 tsp of blue sugar sprinkles

In a long banana split dish, place 2 scoops of vanilla ice cream. Place the sliced bananas along the edge of the two scoups of ice cream. Carefully drizzle the blue cocktail mix over the top of the two scoops of ice cream. Sprinkle with blue sugar sprinkles all over everything. Serve and Enjoy !

Fuchsia Lagoon

Just as spectacular as its blue sister, the Fuchsia Lagoon will really get the little girls excited.

Substitute the blue cocktail mix and blue sprinkles with strawberry or any red cocktail mix and red sugar sprinkles. Serve and Enjoy !

These two ice cream desserts are great for any birthday party, young or not so young !

Pink Princess

Pink is just about every little girl's dream color. So a Pink Princess is perfect for any little princess's special party. Little ice cream dishes just make it all the more special.

You will need 6 little dessert dishes. See photo at right.

1 quart strawberry ice cream or raspberry sherbet
12 pink sugar wafer cookies
pink sugar sprinkles
some whipped topping or strawberry topping
pink cocktail umbrellas or any fun princess accessory, optional but cute

Fill each ice cream dish with strawberry ice cream. Add two cookies on one side. A large dollop of whipped topping and then sprinkle with pink sugar sprinkles. Add the umbrella and serve immediately. Enjoy !

Dark Shadow

Kids love vampire movies and anything with a skull on it. I call this ice cream dessert "Dark Shadows" because it can't get the chocolate any darker and more chocolatey.

You will need 6 cool ice cream dishes, See photo at right.

1 quart chocolate fudge ice cream
one jar hot fudge topping
1/2 cup mini chocolate chips

12 chocolate Oreo cookies
1/2 cup chopped peanuts
handful of pretzel sticks

Place a scoop of chocolate ice cream in each dish. Top with a large spoonful of hot fudge. Sprinkle with mini chocolate chips and chopped peanuts. Place an Oreo cookie on one side and several pretzel sticks on the other. Serve and Enjoy !

Blue Dragon Smoothie

Another fun dessert that will be perfect for the next generation of ice cream lovers. Smooth and delicious and you eat it with a straw, well actually, you drink it ! This recipe will make enough for 3-4 small smoothies.

1 quart blue Smurfs or vanilla ice cream
1 cup whole milk
a few drops of blue food coloring
1 cup of crushed ice

In a blender, add all the ingredients. Blend until smooth and creamy. Serve in tall skinny glasses with a fat straw for a fun presentation. Enjoy !

Molly Madness

Does anyone know a Molly who isn't the cutest and craziest person around ? Every time I make this little sundae I think of her and all her crazy little actions. It is just the cutest little sundae ever. Just ask Molly or any of her crazy friends.

This recipe will make enough for 6 desserts. See photo at right.

1 quart rainbow sherbet (orange will work as well)
1/4 cup multi-colored sprinkles
6 candy sticks or a variety of gum drops or gummy bears

Add a large scoop of sorbet to each ice cream dish. Add the gum drops or gummy bears and then sprinkle with the candy sprinkles. I have even been known to add a large dollop of marshmallow cream before the sprinkles. Serve and Enjoy !

Molly Creamsicle Delight

For Molly's Creamsicle Delight, place a scoup of softened vanilla ice cream in the bottom of a small dessert dish. Add a scoop of orange sherbert and then another scoop of softened vanilla ice cream. Quick and simple, but really delicious. Serve and Enjoy !

Rock Star Sundae

My friends refer to this as "The Stomach Ache". This over the top sundae is perfect for all teenagers who want to experience an overwhelming indulgence of ice cream and all the combination of flavors that go along with it. Not for those who are squeamish or on a diet or worried about appearances. Just go for it !

You will need several different flavors of ice cream. Not the usual ones, but ones like black cherry, rocky road, Smurfs, chocolate mocha and coconut cream.

Several different toppings
some sprinkles
some chopped nuts
whipped cream
maraschino cherries

Fill this oversize sundae dish will 3-4 small scoops of any of your favorite ice creams in different flavors. Pour a different topping over each of the different flavors of ice cream. Sprinkle with chopped nuts and any sprinkles you have. Finish off with a large scoop of whipping cream and a maraschino cherry. Serve immediately and Enjoy !

Banana Split Pizza

If this super sundae doesn't put you over the top, nothing will. It's a great combination of chocolate, bananas, pineapple and strawberries.

You will need 6 banana split dishes. See photo at right.

1 pan of chocolate brownies (8x8)
1 quart vanilla ice cream, softened
3 bananas, sliced
1 cup sliced strawberries
1 cup fresh pineapple pieces
1/2 cup chopped pecans or walnuts
1 jar chocolate topping

You can also use chocolate chips, toffee chips and maraschino cherries.

Cut the brownies in long pieces to fit the bottom of each banana split dish. Add a small scoop of ice cream on top of the brownie and flatten slightly. Top with sliced strawberries, pineapple pieces and bananas. Sprinkle with chopped pecans and drizzle with chocolate syrup. Serve immediately and Enjoy !

INDEX

About the author.

ROBERT ZOLLWEG is a native of Toledo, Ohio and has been entertaining professionally for many years. After a few cookbooks on mini tastings and desserts, writing this cookbook Fountain Shoppe: Fun with Ice Cream was just the natural next step. He has worked in the tabletop industry for over 40 years. He designs glassware, flatware and ceramic

products for the retail and foodservice industry. He has worked with all of the major retailers; Bed Bath & Beyond, Crate and Barrel, Pier One Imports, Williams-Sonoma, Macy's, Cost Plus World Market, JCPenneys, Target, Walmart, Meijers, Home Outfitters and Sears to name a few. He has worked most of his professional career for Libbey Glass in Toledo, Ohio. Robert has traveled the world extensively looking for color and design trends and the right product to design and bring to the retail and foodservice marketplace. He is also an artist-painter in his spare time and works primarily with acrylic on canvass using bold colors. He has always had a passion for entertaining, so this Fountain Shoppe cookbook will continue this passion. He currently lives in his historic home in Toledo's Historic Old West End and in the artistic community of Saugatuck, Michigan.

For more information about Robert and his other cookbooks, visit his web site at www.zollwegart.com

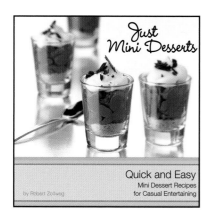

Just Mini Desserts

Quick and Easy
Mini Dessert Recipes
for Casual Entertaining
by Robert Zollweg

Just mini Cocktails

cocktails &
party drinks

Fun & Exciting Cocktail Recipes
for casual entertaining
and tasting parties
by Robert Zollweg

HOME decor
creative ideas with glass

Decorative Accessories
Wedding & Bridal
Holiday Centerpieces
Young & Modern
Craft Ideas
Bed & Bath

Fun & Exciting Home Décor
decorating ideas with
glass centerpieces
by Robert Zollweg

Just Tasting

mini appetizers
soups & salads

Quick and Easy Recipes
mini appetizers soups & salads
for casual entertaining
by Robert Zollweg

CRAFT BREWS
the right glass for the right beer

ales and lagers
beer cocktails
food pairing with craft beers
by Robert Zollweg

Just Baking
mini pies and casseroles

Quick and Easy
Single Serving Recipes
for casual family entertaining
by Robert Zollweg

COOL COCKTAILS
entertaining with fun glassware

cool cocktail recipes
entertaining with cocktails
non-alcoholic recipes
by Robert Zollweg

Just Mini Desserts
Volume 2

Quick and Easy Recipes
more mini dessert recipes
for casual entertaining
by Robert Zollweg

Just Tasting
Volume 2

mini appetizers
soups & salads

Quick and Easy Recipes
more mini appetizers soups & salads
for casual entertaining
by Robert Zollweg

I hope you have enjoyed my Fountain Shoppe cookbook, with all its fun recipes using ice cream.

Any of my other cookbooks or home decor books would be a wonderful compliment to anyone's home entertaining cookbook collection. They are all available at area retailers or on my web site at: www.zollwegart.com

Enjoy ! Robert

127